JUNGLE BOOK FOR KIDS: SCARY ANIMALS OF THE JUNGLE

BABY PROFESSOR

EDUCATION KIDS

Jungles are home to a wide range of animals and plants.

The tiger is the largest species of cats. It's most famous for its unique orange coloring and black and white stripes. Each tiger has a unique set of stripes.

Poison dart frogs
are one of the
most brightly-
colored creatures
on the planet
earth. They
can be found in
trees, as well as
under leaves and
logs and rocks
on the floor of
the forest.

A tapir is a large, herbivorous mammal. Tapirs weigh from 500-700 pounds. They are good swimmers, they use their snout as a snorkel.

The cougar also commonly known as the mountain lion or puma is native to the Americas. Cougars can run up to 80 kilometers per hour and jump as high as 15 feet. They use whistles, screams, squeaks and purrs to communicate.

Piranhas are small to medium sized fish that live in rivers of South America. Piranhas are known for their razor-sharp teeth and relentless bite.

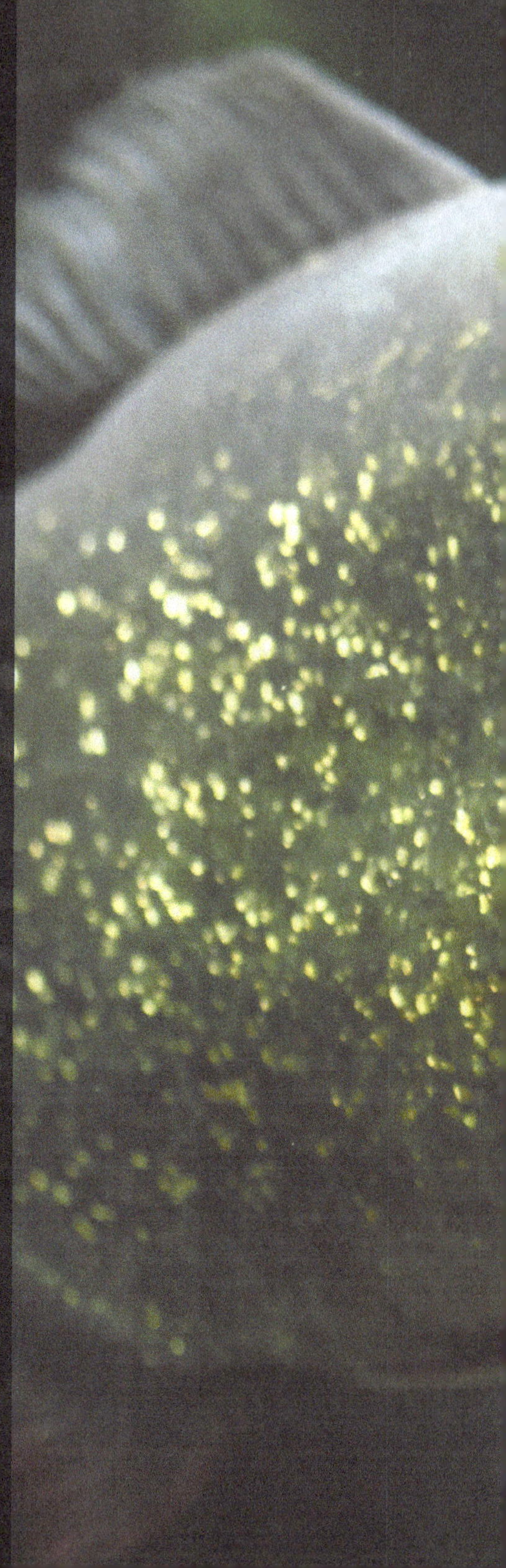

An anaconda is a large snake found in the Amazon jungles of South America. The anaconda is the world's largest snake. It can grow up to 30 feet long.

The Goliath birdeater is the largest spider in the world. These spiders can have a leg span of up to 11 inches. The Goliath bird-eating tarantula has been known to catch young birds.